NUGGETS TO
BECOMING
HER

Angela L. Peterson

Studio Griffin
A Publishing Company
www.studiogriffin.net

For information, contact:
Studio Griffin
A Publishing Company
studiogriffin@outlook.com
www.studiogriffin.net

Cover Design by Ruth E. Griffin
Cover image generated by AI/Adobe

Permission statements for the use of various Bible translations listed in Appendix.

First Edition

ISBN-13: 978-1-954818-50-7

Library of Congress Control Number: 2024919332

1 2 3 4 5 6 7 8 9 10

Dedication

I want to take this opportunity to thank my mom, Barbara Jean Moody, Brown, and recognize the amazing woman she was. Throughout my life she has encouraged me "to become", loved me unconditionally, believed for me, prayed for me, she was patient, kind, and always there for me and my entire family, but most importantly, her desire for us all was to build a personal relationship with our Heavenly Father. Because of her relationship with Jesus, her daily example, and her love, I am who I am today! She is absent yet present.

Introduction

With the purpose of she (me) to understand HER (my true self), I need God's Wisdom. In the Bible, Wisdom is referred to as "Her." As I continue to walk this journey of life with the help of Holy Spirit, I'm finding out daily that I need His Wisdom to BECOME.

Years ago, I had an encounter with God through the scripture John 10:10. At that moment, I realized I wasn't living, I was existing. I, then, began my personal relationship with Jesus. I had received Him as my savior, but not Lord of my life. I initiated researching scriptures, wanting to know Him, wanting to know my heavenly Father, His Son, and Holy Ghost. That's when my journey of "knowing who I am and whose I am" began. In the last few years, Holy Spirit gave me Words of encouragement (through scripture, conversations, social content post, etc.) to strengthen my daily steps. I call them

NUGGETS and began sharing these nuggets in my teachings. It became a "thing!"

My dear friend, Faye Fuller, strongly suggested I put my nuggets in a book for others to gain strength on their journey as well. I procrastinated for about two years. But the more I shared nuggets in my teachings, her suggestion became louder and louder.

I share nuggets with you that have helped me and are helping me heal from my dysfunctional past. These nuggets are not to replace God's Word, but to lead you to it (Bible).

My prayer for the reader: I pray the nuggets encourage you and in return, you encourage someone too! I pray that the scriptures leap off the pages and become alive and medicine to your soul.

For His Glory, I will!

Angela L. Peterson

Nugget

Hiding From It Isn't The Same As Healing From It

I remember living on an emotional roller-coaster. When it was expressed publicly, it was embarrassing for me and the others around me. So, I hid them. I prayed and rebuked them as I was taught. Unfortunately, there were many triggers, and they kept popping out. One day I decided to get off the roller- coaster ride and get on His "healing-ride." Even though the embarrassing emotions popped out, I didn't hide them. Instead, I asked God what to do with them. That's when my emotional healing journey began!

Emotions are important and normal. It would be weird if we didn't have emotions accompanying many of the things we go through in life.

Your emotions should be in the vehicle with you, but they shouldn't have the wheel to your life. In Psalm 103, King David tells his soul (his mind, will, and emotions) to bless the Lord. We can tell our emotions how to behave and walk in the joy of the Lord.

Scripture

I know that you delight to set your truth deep in my spirit. So come into the hidden places of my heart and teach me wisdom.
Psalm 51:6 (TPT)

Nugget

Hard Conversations Must Be Had If You Expect To Grow

One day, I had to have a "hard" conversation with someone (so I thought). When I invited the individual to the conversation, I immediately realized it was a "heart to heart" conversation, not a "hard" one.

Once you build your relationship with Holy Spirit, your vocabulary changes and your insight are no longer yours. You begin to see and respond like Him. So, therefore, when I shared with the individual the type of conversation—heart to heart—that needed to be had, they were at ease.

Scripture

The mouth of the [uncompromisingly] righteous utters wisdom, and his tongue speaks with justice. The law of his God is in his heart; none of his steps shall slide.

Psalms 37:30 (AMPC)

Nugget

The Conversation First Begins With You

When I continued my relationship with Holy Spirit, I saw me. I began to talk to me. So many times, I went to the other individual to confront, get counsel, or simply needing an ear, but when I built this amazing relationship between Jesus and myself, my conversation was had with us first. And usually afterwards there was no other conversation needed to be had with others, or the response was totally different than what I originally planned. Nothing good ever comes from conversations conducted under stress and duress.

Scripture

There is a time to keep silent, and a time to speak.
Ecclesiastes 3:7 (ERV)

Even fools are thought wise if they keep silent,
and discerning if they hold their tongues.
Proverbs 17:28 (NIV)

Nugget
Become Fully Present To The One Who Is Fully Present To You

There were many years in my life where I wasn't present in my day. I was "doing" but not "being." I didn't acknowledge the One who gave me a brand-new day, the strength "to do," or simply thanked Him for life.

However, I did know without Him there was no me. But lived in my feelings. By doing so, I didn't experience God's presence in my day.

Scripture

Because of you, I know the path of life, as I taste the fullness of joy in your presence. At your right side I experience divine pleasures forevermore!
Psalm 16:11 (TPT)

Nugget

Sometimes We're Tested Not To Show Our Weakness, But To Discover Our Strengths

There are times in my life when my weakness shows up and I'm surprised and think, "Why is this happening to me? What's wrong with me? I shouldn't feel this way…" and so forth and so on.

But when I settle my soul and allow Holy Spirit to lead me to truth, revelation is made available: weakness will always be, just as strength is. In my weakness, I rely on God's strength. It is nothing to be afraid or ashamed of. I simply need Jesus in everything I do.

Scripture

But he answered me, "My grace is always more than enough for you, and my power finds its full expression through your weakness." So I will celebrate my weaknesses, for when I'm weak I sense more deeply the mighty power of Christ living in me. So I'm not defeated by my weakness, but delighted! For when I feel my weakness and endure mistreatment—when I'm surrounded with troubles on every side and face persecution because of my love for Christ—I am made yet stronger. For my weakness becomes a portal to God's power.

2 Corinthians 12:9-10 (TPT)

Nugget

To Deal With The Future, You Must Deal With Your Past

After coming to "myself," God revealed who He created me to be, and I began walking towards my destiny. However, it was with insecurities, fear, pain, etc. Triggers from my past kept showing up and I kept pushing them down. But they kept resurfacing.

This time I thought to use God's Word... I cast down every stronghold and told Satan, you are under my feet, I am the head and not the tail.

I asked God, "Why the triggers?" I explained, "I'm reading the Bible, going to church, singing, and worshipping you..."

His response was, "Pushing them down is not the answer for them going away."

Me: But when they come, I feel inadequate, ashamed, vulnerable, and sometimes, it's painful. I don't want to feel it or see it.

God reminded me that just as I spoke His Word, I must believe His Word that He will never leave me nor forsake me. He then comforted me and let me know He is with me in the "fire" of the past, not to hurt me but to heal me for my future. So, no matter how hot my emotions get from the triggers, I know that God is with me!

Scripture

Then King Nebuchadnezzar was astonished; and he rose in haste and spoke, saying to is counselors, "Did we not cast three men bound into the midst of the fire?"
They answered and said to the king, "True, O king."
"Look!" he answered, "I see four men loose, walking in the midst of the fire; and they are not hurt, and the form of the fourth is like the Son of God."
Daniel 3:4-25 (NKJV)

Nugget

No One Needs You Like You Need You

I found myself being there for everyone. I'm a great listener, I'm a firm secret keeper, I love giving gifts, and I will show up where you need me, but you don't know that I'm coming, I love surprising people, showering love on strangers, and the list goes on.

Unfortunately, I didn't do that for myself. Through my relationship with Jesus, I was introduced to me. When I began to care for me, I then realized I needed "ME" to Be.

Scripture

*Above all else, guard your heart, for everything
you do flows from it.*
Proverbs 4:23 (NIV)

Nugget

A Lot Of Us Are In Trouble Based On What We "Know"

I was one of those people who responded to situations based on my natural knowledge, gained from family and friends.

When I received and believed God's Knowledge, I responded differently. I then prayed and asked God to forgive me. It was difficult to forgive myself for the choices I made.

Jesus lifted my head by responding to me, "You didn't know." And that freed me from myself.

Scripture

*For the LORD gives wisdom; from his mouth
comes knowledge and understanding.*
Proverbs 2:6 (NIV)

*Wisdom is a gift from a generous God, and every
word He speaks is full of revelation and becomes a
fountain of understanding within you.*
Proverbs 2:6 (TPT)

Nugget

Address The Fact "My Thinking Has Been Off"

Through reading the Bible, I came to myself (my true self) and realized my thinking was off, based on the pages of God's Word. Then I began to think the way God thought of me and about others the way He thought of them.

Scripture

Finally, brothers and sisters, whatever is true, whatever is noble, whatever is right, whatever is pure, whatever is lovely, whatever is admirable— if anything is excellent or praiseworthy—think about such things.
Philippians 4:8 (NIV)

Nugget
Fear and Faith Open Doors

I stayed paralyzed in fear for many years but had faith that God is. One day, revelation illuminated that faith opens doors of possibility and fear opens doors to impossibility. I can choose to stay paralyzed or walk by faith in freedom.

Fear kept presenting itself, but I kept walking by faith. No longer did fear dictate my steps.

Scripture

For we walk by faith, not by sight.
2 Corinthians 5:7 (NKJV)

Nugget

The Secret To Success Is Hidden In Your Daily Routine

So many see success, but not the process. Just as I began the journey of soul healing, a daily routine had to take place. Little did I know, each day I was stronger than the day before.

Scripture

"If God gives such attention to the appearance of wildflowers—most of which are never even seen— don't you think he'll attend to you, take pride in you, do his best for you? What I'm trying to do here is to get you to relax, to not be so preoccupied with getting, so you can respond to God's giving.

People who don't know God and the way he works fuss over these things, but you know both

God and how he works. Steep your life in God-reality, God-initiative, God-provisions. Don't worry about missing out. You'll find all your everyday human concerns will be met. "Give your entire attention to what God is doing right now, and don't get worked up about what may or may not happen tomorrow. God will help you deal with whatever hard things come up when the time comes.

Matthew 6:30-34 (MSG)

Nugget
What You Heal In Yourself, You Heal In Your Family Line

I was living as if I hadn't received Jesus as my Lord and Savior. I didn't know it then, but when I came to myself and started the journey of healing, my chaos, reactions and responses changed my atmosphere and breathed life to my husband, children and others attached to me.

Scripture

Humiliated, the son finally realized what he was doing, and he thought 'There are many workers at my father's house who have all the food they want with plenty to spare. They lack nothing.

Why am I here dying of hunger, feeding these pigs, and eating their slop?
Luke 15:17 (TPT)

Nugget

The Demons In Your Head Are Not As Powerful As The God In Your Heart

Oh, how I do remember the false voices in my head. Once I established a relationship with Jesus and Holy Spirit, my heart began to heal. I came to know who I was, trained my mind to hear God's voice, not what the enemy was shouting; and with the power of Jesus, I was able to speak with authority to the demon in my head.

Scripture

Little children (believers, dear ones), you are of God, and you belong to Him and have [already] overcome them [the agents of the antichrist];

because He who is in you is greater than he
(Satan) who is in the world [of sinful mankind].
1 John 4:4 (AMP)

Nugget

God's Plan Is Greater Than Our Prospective

When my perspective changed, that's when I was able to yield to God's plan for my life. I had to settle myself (my perspective) to His plan (His perspective). I'm experiencing His plan is far greater than I can imagine.

Scripture

Because we don't focus our attention on what is seen but on what is unseen. For what is seen is temporary, but the unseen realm is eternal.
2 Corinthians 4:18 (TPT)

Nugget

Waiting Is A Gift,
Not A Spiritual Detention

Lisa Harper was speaking at a conference and out of everything she said, this statement illuminated my soul and became a nugget for me:

"Waiting is a gift, not a spiritual detention."

When I waited in the past, it felt like I was drowning, missing out or in trouble. I had a religious mindset of the definition of waiting.

But when my relationship grew in Christ, I asked questions. Why am I here? Did I make this appointment? Did God make this appointment?

When I received the answer, I sought God to what to do while I'm waiting. Just as a doctor's waiting room, you fill out forms, get your measurements, take blood, etc.... You are waiting to see the doctor.

I don't sit in the waiting room wondering why I'm there. Just as I'm waiting for God's manifestation, there is something I can do and something I can learn.

Scripture

The LORD is good to those who wait for him, to the soul who seeks him.
Laminations 3:25 (ESV)

Nugget
Highlight
His Strength

There are seasons in my life when the devil had me dwelling on my weaknesses, which paralyzed me from obeying God's assignments for my life. I was afraid my weakness would appear and very ashamed of them. But thanks be to God I found out it's not about me anyways, it's all about God's strength through me. I was strengthened, encouraged, and drew closer to my Savior.

Scripture

But they who wait for the LORD shall renew their strength; they shall mount up with wings

like eagles; they shall run and not be weary; they
shall walk and not faint.
Isaiah 40:31 (ESV)

Nugget

Healing Is A Process,
Not An Event

Surprisingly, there are times in my life hurt from my past shows up. I asked myself, why are you here? What's wrong with me? Why am I feeling this way?

The human mind stores memories and can show up anytime. However, healing is a daily process to deal with the past. Religion had me believe once you've prayed about it, it's gone, but relationship with God allowed me to totally depend on Him to heal me daily.

Scripture

I depend on God alone; I put my hope in him. He alone protects and saves me; he is my defender, and I shall never be defeated. My salvation and honor depend on God; he is my strong protector; he is my shelter. Trust in God at all times, my people. Tell him all your troubles, for he is our refuge.

Psalms 62:5-12 (GNT)

Nugget

Acknowledge The One
Who Made The Day
Before You Start Your Day

When I read this quote on Instagram, I immediately jotted it down for my nugget to become *"HER."* Every day when I wake up, I talk to the One who watched over me while I slept and woke me up to New Mercy. I include Him in the conversation and acknowledge that I cannot do the day without Him. I want to see Him in my day, and I want others to see Him through me.

It took years to get to this point. I used to wake up and rely on my own strength and as a result, my day would be miserable.

I'm thankful to God for His patience for me. He knew if I kept seeking His face, I would end up here.

Scripture

The LORD replied, "My Presence will go with you, and I will give you rest."
Exodus 33:14 (NIV)

Nugget

Don't Put Your Ear To The Wrong Voice

Raising my children at an early age, I put my ear to voices of others for advice. When I began a relationship with God, I came to know Him, not only as my savior, but the Lord of my life and a Father. I went to Him for guidance on how to raise my children. His voice released wisdom and knowledge and brought a peace that healed my brokenness. God taught me how to be a godly mother, and for that, I thank Him.

Scripture

My son, if you accept my words and store up my commands within you, turning your ear to

wisdom and applying your heart to understanding—indeed, if you call out for insight and cry aloud for understanding, and if you look for it as for silver and search for it as for hidden treasure, then you will understand the fear of the LORD and find the knowledge of God.
Proverbs 2:1–5 (NIV)

Nugget

I Can, But The Question Is, Will I?

There's been times in my life when I knew I was capable of the assignment, but fear of the unknown, insecurities and self-doubt stopped me from doing so. I had great ideas and a Word from God, but the question was, will I do it?

As my relationship grew with Jesus, it enabled me to rely in His strength instead of my own. Yes, I was afraid and insecure with self-doubt? But because I no longer depended on what I could do, but what he can do through me, I did it!

Scripture

*I can do all things [which He has called me to do]
through Him who strengthens and empowers
me [to fulfill His purpose—I am self-sufficient in
Christ's sufficiency; I am ready for anything and
equal to anything through Him who infuses me
with inner strength and confident peace.]
Philippians 4:13* (AMP)

Nugget

On This Journey, We Need God's Revelation, Not Our Natural Information

My decisions were once led by natural information and the results were not a success. When I settled myself in God's revelation, began to acknowledge His way, and allow Him to lead my path, revelation was made available to me. I resisted on some occasions, and didn't always follow, but I can testify God's leading is a great success.

Scripture

Trust in and rely confidently on the LORD with all your heart And do not rely on your own insight or understanding. In all your ways know

and acknowledge and recognize Him, And He
will make your paths straight and smooth
[removing obstacles that block your way].
Proverbs 3:5–6 (AMP)

Nugget

When You Know The Light Comes On, You Approach The Darkness Differently
(Tony Peterson)

My husband spoke these words in one of his teachings, and I grabbed onto it and couldn't let it go! And of course, it became one of my nuggets.

I remember approaching my dark situation based on what I couldn't see. One day that same dark situation appeared again, but this time, I approached it with His sight and wisdom, which illuminated my path.

Scripture

*Your word is a lamp to my feet
and a light to my path.
Psalms 119:105* (NIV)

Nugget

The Strength In Any Believer's Life Will Be Found In The Place Of Intimacy With God

On this journey of life, unforeseen things happen. There are several situations that come to mind. However, I will focus on one…

When our son was diagnosed with meningitis and a few other diseases, he was hospitalized for several weeks. Hearing the daily reports from the doctors, seeing his failing results, we felt heavy-hearted and helpless because we couldn't do anything in our power to help him. My strength was found in my worship to God. Then I was led to prayer through which I received supernatural strength and peace. God's strength literally overshadowed me. During this season, I experienced a dry place where it seemed there was no hope.

Scripture

You, God, are my God, earnestly I seek you; I thirst for you, my whole being longs for you, in a dry and parched land where there is no water. I have seen you in the sanctuary and beheld your power and your glory. Because your love is better than life, my lips will glorify you. I will praise you as long as I live, and in your name I will lift up my hands. I will be fully satisfied as with the richest of foods; with singing lips my mouth will praise you. On my bed I remember you; I think of you through the watches of the night. Because you are my help, I sing in the shadow of your wings. I cling to you; your right hand upholds me.
Psalms 63:1–8 (NIV)

Nugget

Your Place (God)
Or Mine (Me)

For years, I lived in "my place" (my mindset). Occasionally, I'd peak out to "His place" (His way of thinking) and sporadically renew my mind with God's word. I realized His place was better than mine.

Scripture

Do not conform to the pattern of this world but be transformed by the renewing of your mind. Then you will be able to test and approve what God's will is—his good, pleasing, and perfect will.
Romans 12:2 (NIV)

Nugget

We Live Wrong Because We Believe Wrong

Oh… I believed wrong for so many years. I believed what the devil told me about myself. So, I lived out the lies of not good enough, not smart enough, not pretty enough, etc. Which then paralyzed me from living!

Mobility came when I began to read, study and meditate on God's Word. His Word began to shine truth on the lies I believed. Then I began to believe what God said about me and in doing so, began to live right instead of wrong.

Scripture

I praise you because I am fearfully and wonderfully made; your works are wonderful, I know that full well. My frame was not hidden from you when I was made in the secret place, when I was woven together in the depths of the earth. Your eyes saw my unformed body; all the days ordained for me were written in your book before one of them came to be.

Psalms 139:14–16 (NIV)

Nugget

You Can Stay Where You Are
Or Live Where You Belong

After receiving and believing in God's Truth about me, I had to decide to either stay where I was or live where I belong. I chose to live where I belong.

Scripture

I have been crucified with Christ and I no longer live, but Christ lives in me. The life I now live in the body, I live by faith in the Son of God, who loved me and gave himself for me.
Galatians 2:20 (NIV)

Nugget

If We Keep Bringing Bricks From Our Past, We Will Build The Same House In A Different Location

My family and I relocated several times. Each home, city, and state we relocated to, I carried my past with me. Location didn't change me, God changed me. There were a lot of bricks to knock down but with the help of Holy Spirit, I'm building a new home by His blueprints.

Scripture

"Everyone then who hears these words of mine and does them will be like a wise man who built his house on the rock. And the rain fell, and the

floods came, and the winds blew and beat on that house, but it did not fall, because it had been founded on the rock. And everyone who hears these words of mine and does not do them will be like a foolish man who built his house on the sand. And the rain fell, and the floods came, and the winds blew and beat against that house, and it fell, and great was the fall of it."
Matthew 7:24-27 (ESV)

Nugget

It Doesn't Mean
The Damage Never Existed,
It Means The Damage
No Longer Controls You

I've heard people say forgive and forget. I tried that "religious" way of living, but I was miserable. Why? Because God created intelligent humans. Our brain stores memory. So, therefore, we ought not forget. We can forgive with the help of Holy Spirit. And we can allow God to heal us from the damage. Our thought process will be in control over it.

Scripture

And after you have suffered a little while, the God of all grace, who has called you to his eternal glory in Christ, will himself restore, confirm, strengthen, and establish you.
1 Peter 5:10 (ESV)

Nugget

Don't Just Show Up To Church, Show Up To Jesus

I was born into church (organization/building) and we faithfully attended every Sunday, mid-week and volunteer ministry service. We were taught that coming to the building every time the doors opened was being faithful to God. I was raised believing that the church building brought me freedom, peace, and righteousness. So, I showed up to all the services.

Of course, I participated where there was a need. Of course, I wanted to have freedom, peace, and righteousness. Of course, that's the only place I read the Bible. Why? Because I was taught that's where you show up to hear

God, praise God, serve God, and you become righteous.

Wrong. Wrong. Wrong.

When I began a relationship with Jesus, that's when I discovered I am His dwelling place (church). So wherever, I go, He is with me. I can read the Bible at home, I can pray to God for myself, I can experience His presence in my home, I can be His hands and feet in my community, etc.

The more I showed up to Jesus, the more He showed up to me and the more I wanted to show up. He was and is my daily bread. I didn't have to wait to get to church to get fed. Now with the Knowledge and Under-standing of Holy Spirit, when I enter the doors of a church, His presence enters in with me. It's a great celebration with other believers!

Scripture

[Do you not know and understand that you [the church] are the temple of God, and that the Spirit of God dwells [permanently] in you [collectively and individually]?
I Corinthians 3:16 (AMP)

Declarations

Inspired and written by my husband, Tony Peterson, pastor of Every Walk of Life Ministries.

It's important to declare God's Word into the atmosphere. I share these declarations to add to your nuggets because I want you to be full of 'HER (Wisdom).'

Fearfully, Wonderfully Made Confessions

Heavenly Father, I thank You that my life is Your very breath in human form. Your best material is in me. I'm a product of Your love. I am destined for greatness, crowned with the glory and honor to have dominion over all Your works. I thank you, God, for making me so mysteriously complex! Everything you do is marvelously breathtaking.

Thank You, Lord, I have had a rebirth of my God-worth. Knowing that I am created in Your image and likeness reminds me of my divine origin, purpose, and infinite value. I shall never again depreciate the "one" that You value so much. I shall never again put down what You have lifted, I am vital because of Your designed plan for me.

Father, my heritage is to have Your best, to enjoy Your companionship and to use Your wealth and power for the good of Your Kingdom and others. I am created for life, love, power, prosperity, success, and dignity. Seeds of greatness are in me. You have planned life's best for me as Your child even before the foundations of the world.

Father God, I declare Psalms 119:14 over my life and the lives of my sisters from this day forward. I praise you because I am Your unique creation, and I am awesome! You have approached even the smallest details of my being with excellence. I am the royal works of Your hands, "Fearfully and wonderfully made" and it simply amazes me to think about it; I carry this knowledge deep within my soul and I thank You for it.

God, I shall no longer discredit, demean, or destroy what You have created in Your own image. Father, I thank you for Your Holy Spirit, Who reminds me of my purpose and of the Love You have for me. You have blessed me to complete every project I take on and every assignment I begin. You have equipped me to share the Goodness of Your Grace with others and live victorious in this life and the life to come!

Thank you that an outpouring of the Holy Spirit, wisdom, truth, love, joy, peace, righteousness, faith, holiness, and your Word will saturate me TODAY. Father, I thank you that Your Word will not return void but shall accomplish everything it is sent out to perform, in Jesus' name. Amen!

Authentic Self Confessions

Heavenly Father, I thank You that my life is Your words spoken into existence. Your best material is in me. I'm a product of Your unwavering love. I am destined for greatness; I walk in the beauty & strength You have lavished upon me. My identity, my true self, lines up with all You have called me to be. I thank you, God, for making me so genuinely extraordinary! Everything you do is marvelously breathtaking.

Thank You, Lord, I have had a re-awakening of my irreplaceable worth. Knowing that I am created in Your image and likeness reminds me of my divine origin, purpose, and infinite value. I shall never again depreciate my individuality, something You value so highly. I shall never again put down what You have lifted. I am vital because of Your excellent plan for me, which was spoken before the foundations of the world.

Father, my birthright is to have Your best; to distribute Your wealth and power for the good of Your Kingdom and others. I am created for life, love, power, prosperity, success, and dignity. Whether on a mountaintop or in our special garden, Your companionship nourishes me, it quenches my thirsty soul.

Father God, I declare Philippians 4:8 over my life and the lives of my sisters from this day forward. I praise you because I am Your exceptional creation, and I am awesome! I will keep my thoughts continually fixed on all that is authentic and real; honorable and admirable, beautiful and respectful, pure and holy, merciful and kind. For You are the reason that "excellence" is unfolding in my life, and I praise You for it!

God, I shall no longer discredit, degrade, or destroy what You have purposefully designed in Your own image. Father, I thank You for Your Holy Spirit, Who reminds me of my uniqueness and of the Love You have for me. You have graced me with talents, gifts & abilities to complete every project I take on and every assignment I begin. You have equipped me to be my "Authentic Self" and live victorious in this life and the life to come!

Thank you that an outpouring of the Holy Spirit, wisdom, truth, love, joy, peace, righteousness, faith, holiness, and your Word will saturate me TODAY. Father, I thank you that Your Word will not return void but shall accomplish everything it is sent out to perform, in Jesus' name. Amen!

Anchored Soul Confessions

Heavenly Father, I recognize my value, that You created me in Your image and likeness.

My life is Your very breath in human form. Your best material is in me. I'm a product of Your love. I am destined for greatness, crowned with the glory and honor to have dominion over all Your works.

Thank You, Lord, I have had a rebirth of my God-worth. Knowing that I am created in Your image and likeness reminds me of my divine origin, purpose, and infinite value. I shall never again depreciate the "one" that You value so much. I shall never again put down what You have lifted up, I am vital because of Your designed plan for me.

Father, my heritage is to have Your best, to enjoy Your companionship and to use Your wealth and power for the good of Your Kingdom and others. I am created for life, love, power, prosperity, success, and dignity. Seeds of greatness are in me. I know that You have planned life's best for me as Your child before the foundation of the world.

God, I shall no longer discredit, demean, or destroy what You have created in Your own image. Father, I thank you for Your Holy Spirit, Who reminds me of my purpose and of the Love You have for me. You have blessed me to complete every project I take on and every assignment I begin. You have equipped me to share the Goodness of Your Grace with others and live victorious in this life and the life to come!

Father God, I declare Hebrews 6:19 over my life and the lives of my sisters. The Hope we have is like a strong, unbreakable anchor holding our souls to You. Regardless of the "storms & seas" of circumstances that face us, we walk in the grace, strength, and stability of our "Anchored Soul" because our trust is in You.

Thank you that an outpouring of the Holy Spirit, wisdom, truth, love, joy, peace, righteousness, faith, holiness, and your Word will saturate me TODAY. Father, I thank you that Your Word will not return void but shall accomplish everything it is sent out to perform, in Jesus' name. Amen!

She Becomes HER

Heavenly Father, I thank You that even before this world was formed, Your plans of goodness for me and a bright future for my life were already laid out. You continue to reveal more of Who You really are to me and for that, I am grateful. I'm a product of Your extravagant love and it strengthens me to face everything that comes my way. As I walk the Life path you've given me, my hunger for Your Wisdom grows and I begin to discover who I am becoming.

Thank You, Lord, for giving me the desire to pursue You in every way! Wisdom has sent out a clarion call and she is drawing me. She is loud, clear and is stirring me to follow the deeper things of You. I am eager to follow because You pour blessings upon those who find her. As wisdom increases within me, great treasures are revealed in my life which expands Your kingdom.

Father God, I declare Proverbs 3:17 over my life and the lives of my sisters from this day forward. I declare that we are living in your ways of wisdom, and it is a sweet life! It is a life that is full and prosperous in all facets, overflowing in righteousness. We are convinced and sure that You designed an existence for us that is always drawing us into a place of wholeness and unity.

God, I will no longer deprive myself from or spoil my "spiritual appetite" for the wisdom you have with certainty prepared for me to enjoy. Father, I thank You for Holy Spirit, Who constantly reminds me of the benefits of attaining wisdom. He prompts me to **Hear Your Word**, which has the power to **Erase my past** so I can wisely **Respond to my future**. There is no doubt that You have fully equipped me to become "H.E.R".

Resources

Here's a few resources to help you become HER!

Bridging The Gap. Dana Fuller. Studio Griffin, LLC. 2020.

Cleaning Up Your Mental Mess: 5 Simple, Scientifically Proven Steps to Reduce Anxiety, Stress, and Toxic. Dr. Caroline Leaf. Baker Books. 2021

Rest For The Soul: 30-Day Devotional. Shawanda Williams. Cocoon to Wings Publishing. 2020.

The Garden Within: Where the War with Your Emotions Ends and Your Most Powerful Life Begins. Dr. Anita Phillips. Thomas Nelson. 2023

Appendix

Scriptures marked AMP are taken from the Amplified Bible: Copyright © 2015 by The Lockman Foundation. Used by permission. lockman.org

Scriptures marked AMPC are taken from the Amplified Bible Classic. Copyright © 1954, 1958, 1962, 1964, 1965, 1987 by The Lockman Foundation. Used by permission. lockman.org"

Scriptures marked ESV are taken from the The Holy Bible, English Standard Version: Copyright© 2001 by Crossway, a publishing ministry of Good News Publishers. Used by permission.

Scriptures marked ERV are taken from the Holy Bible: Easy-to-Read Version, International Edition. © 2013, 2016 by Bible

Acknowledgements

I acknowledge my husband, Tony Peterson. He married me as a broken young lady and gave me proper space to heal. This allowed me to become who God created me to be. He speaks life and truth into my soul, he supports me, he prays for me, he believes in me, he loves me, he blesses me, and he nourishes me in so many ways. I'm blessed beyond measure for a Godly man. I know he was called by God to serve me.

I also acknowledge my children Tarsheila, Durrrell and CJ. They were part of my healing journey. They didn't know the depths of it, but the parts they did see they loved me, they forgave me, and they believed the God in me.

These nuggets are written for my generation, their generation, and generations to come.

About The Author

Angela shares the Word of God in such an authentic way that every woman receives the understanding to "Live the Word". Her desire is to enlighten all women, that God has a purpose and a destiny for their lives. (Jeremiah 29:11).

The Creator has called her, to proclaim to all women "who they are and who's they are". She believes many women have given up "ground" to the enemy on the battlefield of circumstances, setbacks or compromise. Her passion is to assist them into tapping into the power and authority of God's Wisdom for their lives. (Proverbs 3:13-18).

Angela is the founder of "Table Talk with Pastor Angela" (The women's ministry of Every Walk of Life Ministries). She holds an associate's degree in early childhood education, bachelor's degree in Elementary / Middle School and a master's degree in administration Christian education.

Angela and her husband Tony, of thirty-four years, pastor Every Walk of Life Ministries. She's the mother to her amazing children, daughter TarSheila and son-in-love David, son Durrell and daughter-in-love Jade, and son Colton "CJ" James. She's also a proud "Honey" of three grandchildren (a.k.a. "the cubs"). She believes family is her "first ministry". The Peterson's currently reside in the Greater Tampa Bay Area.